Oregon

STATE OF OREGON

1859

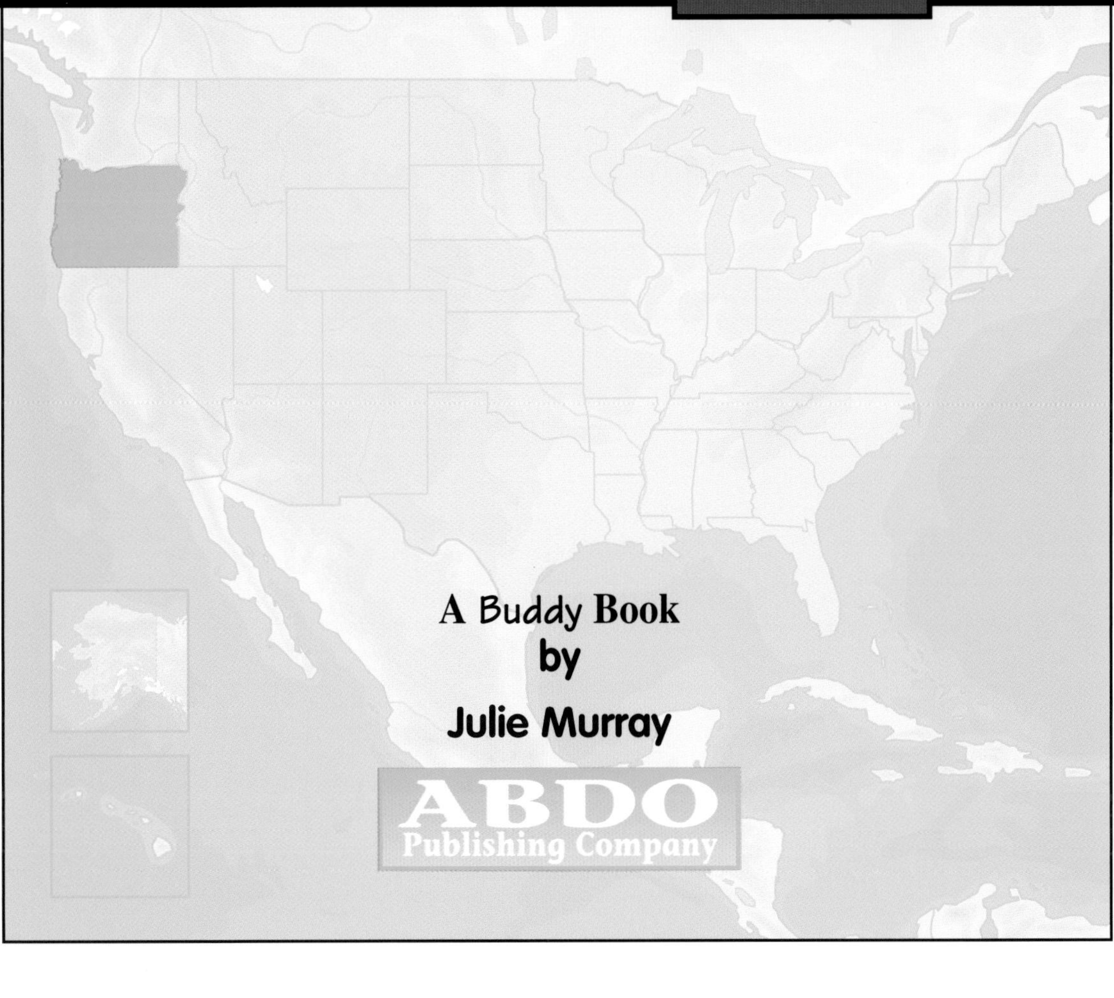

A Buddy Book
by
Julie Murray

ABDO
Publishing Company

VISIT US AT

www.abdopub.com

Published by ABDO Publishing Company, 4940 Viking Drive, Edina, Minnesota 55435.

Printed in the United States.

Edited by: Sarah Tieck
Contributing Editor: Michael P. Goecke
Graphic Design: Deb Coldiron, Maria Hosley
Image Research: Sarah Tieck
Photographs: Clipart.com, Corbis, Digital Vision, Eyewire, Getty Images, Library of Congress, One Mile Up, Photodisc

Library of Congress Cataloging-in-Publication Data

Murray, Julie, 1969-
  Oregon / Julie Murray.
    p. cm. — (The United States)
  Includes index.
    Contents: A snapshot of Oregon — Where is Oregon? — All about Oregon — Cities and the capital — Famous citizens — The landscape of Oregon — The Oregon Trail — Crater Lake National Park — A history of Oregon.
  ISBN 1-59197-696-0
    1. Oregon—Juvenile literature. I. Title.

F876.3.M87 2005
979.5—dc22

                                                    2005047827

Table Of Contents

A Snapshot Of Oregon

Oregon is known for its forests. About half of the state is covered in forests. And, the state is a leader in lumber production. Oregon's landscape also includes majestic Mount Hood, crystal clear Crater Lake, and the rugged Pacific coast.

Oregon is known for its scenic landscape.

There are 50 states in the United States. Every state is different. Every state has an official nickname. Oregon's state nickname is "The Beaver State." This is because Oregon's early settlers trapped beavers for their prized fur. Today, the American beaver is the state's official animal.

Oregon became the 33rd state on February 14, 1859. Today, Oregon is the 10th-largest state in America. It has 97,052 square miles (251,364 sq km) of land. Oregon is home to 3,421,399 people.

A waterfall in one of Oregon's forests.

Where Is Oregon?

There are four parts of the United States. Each part is called a region. Each region is in a different area of the country. The United States Census Bureau says the four regions are the Northeast, the South, the Midwest, and the West.

Oregon borders the Pacific Ocean.

Oregon is located in the West region of the United States. Oregon's temperatures are cool and mild.

Four Regions of the United States of America

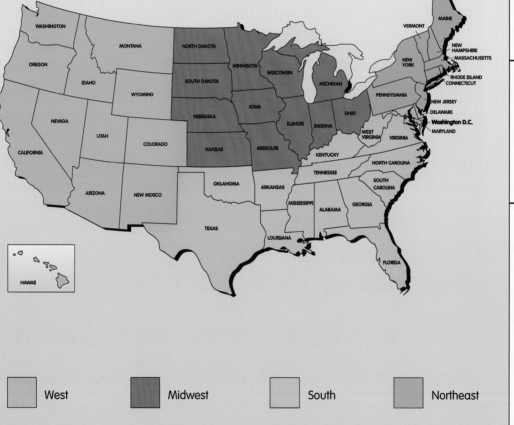

West   Midwest   South   Northeast

Oregon is bordered by four states, two rivers, and an ocean. The Columbia River and the state of Washington make up Oregon's northern border. The Snake River and the state of Idaho are east. Nevada and California are south. The Pacific Ocean forms Oregon's western border.

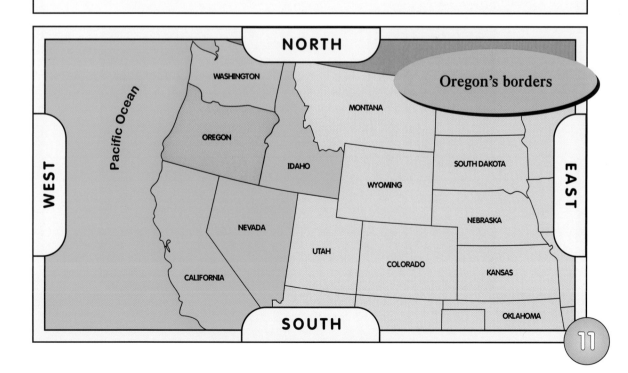

NORTH

WASHINGTON

Oregon's borders

MONTANA

Pacific Ocean

OREGON

IDAHO

SOUTH DAKOTA

WYOMING

WEST

EAST

NEVADA

NEBRASKA

UTAH

COLORADO

KANSAS

CALIFORNIA

OKLAHOMA

SOUTH

Oregon

State abbreviation: OR

State nickname: The Beaver State

State capital: Salem

State motto: She Flies With Her Own Wings

Statehood: February 14, 1859, 33rd state

Population: 3,421,399, ranks 28th

State flag:
Adopted in 1925

Land area: 97,052 square miles (251,364 sq km), ranks 10th

State song: "Oregon, My Oregon"

State government: Three branches: legislative, executive, and judicial

Average July temperature: 66°F (19°C)

Average January temperature: 32°F (0°C)

State flower:
Oregon grape

State bird:
Western meadowlark

State tree:
Douglas fir

13

Cities And The Capital

Salem is the capital city of Oregon. Salem became the state capital in 1851. This city is home to Willamette University. It is located in Oregon's Willamette Valley. Willamette University is one of the oldest universities in the western United States.

Sunset over Willamette Valley.

A view of Portland.

Portland is the largest city in Oregon. It is located in the northwestern part of the state, where the Columbia and Willamette Rivers meet.

Portland is a city full of beautiful outdoor spaces. Sometimes it is called the "City of Roses." This is because of all the roses that blossom there.

Famous Citizens

John McLoughlin (1784–1857)

John McLoughlin was born in Canada in 1784. Still, he is known as the "Father of Oregon." He was a partner in a fur-trading company called the North West Company. He had an important role in developing the Oregon Territory. He encouraged people to settle there. And, he made friends with the Native Americans.

John McLoughlin

Famous Citizens

Matt Groening (1954–)

Matt Groening was born in Portland. He is a cartoonist. He created a famous television cartoon called *The Simpsons*. It started in 1987. Groening named the characters in the show after people in his own family.

Matt Groening

The Landscape Of Oregon

Oregon is known for its beautiful scenery. This state has mountains, waterfalls, lakes, cliffs, coasts, and forests.

The western edge of Oregon is on the Pacific Ocean. Oregon has 296 miles (476 km) of coastline. This area has sandy beaches, steep cliffs, and rocky shorelines. Mountains rise up from the shoreline. These mountains are called the Coast Range. They are full of dense forests.

Sunset on the Pacific Ocean.

A view of Oregon's coast.

A view of Mount Hood.

Just east of the coastal region is the Willamette Valley. This is where the major cities in Oregon are located. The Willamette Valley has rich farmland. On the eastern side of the Willamette Valley is the Cascade Range. This is where Mount Hood is located. It is the tallest point in Oregon. It stands 11,239 feet (3,426 m) high.

Much of eastern Oregon is high flatland with ranches and farms. This area is called the Columbia Plateau. There are also mountain ranges in this area.

Hells Canyon and the Snake River are found along the border between Oregon and Idaho. Hells Canyon is the deepest gorge in the United States. It is more than one mile (two km) deep. It is deeper than the Grand Canyon. People go hiking and white-water rafting in the gorge of Hells Canyon.

The Oregon Trail

Thousands of pioneers headed west in the 1800s. Back then, the western part of the United States was a great wilderness. In the early 1840s, people began to hear about the rich land and opportunities in Oregon.

Many people traveled west on the Oregon Trail. The Oregon Trail extended from Missouri to Oregon.

A stone marker on the Oregon Trail.

These men, women, and children traveled in covered wagons. They made their way across the United States. Buffalo herds roamed the land.

Life along the Oregon Trail was hard. The journey took about six to eight months. The pioneers faced sickness, disease, hunger, and cold weather. Many people died along the trail.

Most of the pioneers who traveled all the way to Oregon settled in the Willamette Valley.

Crater Lake
National Park

Crater Lake National Park opened in 1902. It is Oregon's only national park.

A view of Crater Lake.

People visit Crater Lake to hike, camp, fish, and cross-country ski.

Crater Lake National Park is located in the southern part of the Cascade Range. It has about 180,000 acres (72,843 ha) of wilderness to explore.

Crater Lake National Park is home to the deepest lake in the United States. This is Crater Lake. Crater Lake is 1,932 feet (589 m) deep. It is part of Mount Mazama. Mount Mazama is an inactive volcano.

The lake was created many years ago when the top part of Mount Mazama fell in after erupting. Over the years, water filled this area, and it became a lake. Today, the water in Crater Lake is crystal clear.

Oregon

1543: Spanish explorers sail along Oregon's coast. They are the first Europeans to see Oregon.

1579: Sir Francis Drake sails along parts of Oregon's coast.

1792: Captain Robert Gray explores the Columbia River area of Oregon.

William Clark

1805: Meriwether Lewis and William Clark arrive in Oregon.

1843: Settlers come to Oregon on the Oregon Trail.

1859: Oregon becomes the 33rd state on February 14.

1912: Oregon allows women to vote. Abigail Jane Scott Duniway of Portland helped make this happen.

Meriwether Lewis

1938: Bonneville Dam opens. This produces power and allows ships to travel on the Columbia River.

1948: Mills End Park opens in Portland. This 452-square-inch (2,916-sq-cm) park is the world's smallest.

1991: Barbara Roberts is the first woman to be governor of Oregon.

2004: Oregon celebrates its 145th anniversary.

Cities In Oregon

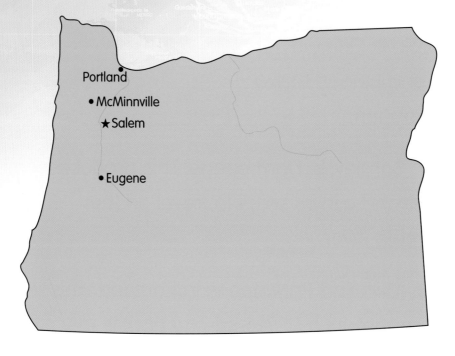

Portland

• McMinnville

★ Salem

• Eugene

Important Words

capital a city where government leaders meet.

gorge a deep, narrow passage between high cliffs.

nickname a name that describes something special
about a person or a place.

pioneers people who traveled across the United
States in the 1800s to settle the western
United States.

plateau a flat-topped mountain.

wilderness wild, unsettled land.

Web Sites

To learn more about Oregon, visit ABDO Publishing Company on the
World Wide Web. Web site links about Oregon are featured on our Book
Links page. These links are routinely monitored and updated to provide
the most current information available.

www.abdopub.com

Index